Mother's Day

BY ANN HEINRICHS • ILLUSTRATED BY R. W. ALLEY

Published by The Child's World®
1980 Lookout Drive • Mankato, MN 56003-1705
800-599-READ • www.childsworld.com

Acknowledgments
The Child's World®: Mary Berendes, Publishing Director
The Design Lab: Design
Jody Jensen Shaffer: Editing

ISBN 9781623235109
LCCN 2013931405

Printed in the United States of America
Mankato, MN
March, 2014
PA02227

ABOUT THE AUTHOR

Ann Heinrichs lives in Chicago, Illinois.
She has written more than two hundred
books for children. She loves traveling
to faraway places.

ABOUT THE ILLUSTRATOR

R. W. Alley enjoys drawing pictures of
happy families from his home in Rhode
Island. He's guided in this effort by his
winsome wife and two cheery children.

Table of Contents

CHAPTER 1

Happy Mother's Day!

Who ran to help me
  when I fell,
And would some pretty
  story tell,
Or kiss the place
  to make it well?
My Mother.

—"My Mother" by Ann Taylor

What do you call your mother? Mother, Mama, Mommy, or Mom? Whatever you call her, she's very special. That's why we have a holiday just for her. It's Mother's Day!

That day, we thank mothers for all they do. We also celebrate those who are like mothers to us. They may be grandmothers, aunts, **stepmothers**, or sisters.

Mother's Day is a time to show mothers how much we love them.

What's the best way to say "Happy Mother's Day"? Just say, "I love you!"

> **A man's work is from sun to sun, but a mother's work is never done.**
>
> —Author unknown

Ancient Romans used music and dance to celebrate Cybele.

CHAPTER 2

Celebrating Motherhood

Many **ancient** religions had a mother **goddess**. Her festivals were often in the spring. Crops were sprouting then. And flowers were bursting into bloom. It was a time to rejoice in new life.

Ancient Romans honored Cybele (SIH-buh-lee). They saw her as the mother of the gods. Cybele's festival took place in March. Dancers whirled around as the music played. We may not celebrate so wildly today. But we still honor our mothers!

CHAPTER 3

A Sunday for Mothers

Mothering Sunday is the fourth Sunday during Lent. Lent is a **traditional** Christian season before Easter.

Mothering Sunday began long ago in England. Poor children often lived away from home. They worked as servants for rich people.

Every spring, servants got a day off. They were to attend their mother church. That was the church in their hometown. The day was called Mothering Sunday.

Children looked forward to Mothering Sunday. They missed their families. And they really missed their mothers!

Mothering Sunday was an early version of Mother's Day.

The children hurried down the sunny lanes. Along the way, they stopped to pick wildflowers. Why? To give to their mothers! In time, Mothering Sunday became a holiday to honor mothers.

A mother's arms are made of tenderness, and children sleep soundly in them.

—Victor Hugo (1802–1885)

Of all the special joys in life,
The big ones and the small,
A mother's love and
   tenderness
Is the greatest of them all.

—Author unknown

Anna Jarvis helped make Mother's Day a national holiday.

CHAPTER 4

How Did Mother's Day Begin?

What about our own Mother's Day? It began with Anna Jarvis.

Anna dearly loved her mother. Her mother had started a women's club. Its members helped the sick. They believed in kindness and peace.

Sadly, Anna's mother died in 1905. Anna wanted to honor her mother. She worked hard to create a mothers' holiday. At last, Anna's dream came true. Mother's Day became a **national** holiday in 1914!

CHAPTER 5

How Do We Celebrate?

Once upon a memory
Someone wiped away a tear,
Held me close and loved me—
Thank you, Mother dear.

—*Author unknown*

We celebrate Mother's Day by showing moms how much we love them.

There are many Mother's Day traditions. We may give our mother a greeting card. Mother's Day cards are very pretty. Inside is a special, loving message. We might give her flowers, too. Candy is another favorite gift. It shows how sweet she is!

Many people wear a **carnation** on Mother's Day. A red or pink carnation means the mother is living. A white carnation means she has died. But a child's love for her lives on.

Cards, candy, flowers, and kisses are all good Mother's Day gifts!

My mother had a great deal of trouble with me, but I think she enjoyed it.

—Mark Twain (1835–1910)

U.S. presidents often wrote about their respect and admiration for their mothers.

CHAPTER 6

Presidents and Their Mothers

My mother was the most beautiful woman
I ever saw. All I am I owe to my mother.

—*George Washington, first president*

There never was a woman like her. She was
gentle as a dove and brave as a lioness.

—*Andrew Jackson, seventh president*

All that I am or ever hope to be,
I owe to my angel mother.

—*Abraham Lincoln, sixteenth president*

No mother has an easy time, {and}
most mothers have very hard times.
—*Theodore Roosevelt, twenty-sixth president*

U.S. presidents were first
their mothers' sons!

Former president Harry Truman knew how special mothers are.

No one in the world can take
the place of your mother. Right or wrong,
from her viewpoint you are always right.
—*Harry Truman, thirty-third president*

CHAPTER 7

Mother's Day around the World

God could not be everywhere, so he created mothers.

—Jewish **proverb**

In France, mothers celebrate their special day with a cake that looks like flowers.

Many countries honor mothers on a special day. In Mexico, Mother's Day is *Día de las Madres* (DEE-ah day lahs MAH-drays). It's always on May 10. Schoolchildren put on dance shows for their mothers. Then everyone enjoys a big meal.

Mother's Day in France is *Fête des Mères* (FEHT day MEHR). It falls on the last Sunday in May. Families gather for a holiday dinner. Then they give Mother a beautiful cake. It's decorated to look like flowers!

In Serbia, children get gifts on Mother's Day!

Serbian people in Eastern Europe celebrate *Materice* (mah-tehr-EET-say). It's the second Sunday before Christmas. That morning, children tiptoe into their mother's bedroom. They gently tie her up. Then they say, "Mother's Day, Mother's Day. What will you pay to get away?" She promises them gifts she has hidden under her pillow. Giggling with delight, they set her free!

CHAPTER 8

Poetry Corner

THE HAND THAT ROCKS THE CRADLE
IS THE HAND THAT RULES THE WORLD

Blessings on the hand of women!

Angels guard its strength and grace,

In the palace, cottage, hovel,

Oh, no matter where the place;

Would that never storms assailed it,

Rainbows ever gently curled;

For the hand that rocks the cradle

Is the hand that rules the world.

—*William Ross Wallace (1819–1881)*

THE READING MOTHER

You may have **tangible** wealth untold;

Caskets of jewels and coffers of gold.

Richer than I you can never be—

I had a Mother who read to me.

—*Strickland Gillilan (1869–1954)*

A MOTHER'S LOVE

A Mother's love is something
That no one can explain,
It is made of deep devotion
And of sacrifice and pain,
It is endless and unselfish
And enduring come what may
For nothing can destroy it
Or take that love away.

—Helen Steiner Rice (1900–1981)

MOTHER

You filled my days with rainbow lights,

Fairy tales and sweet dream nights,

A kiss to wipe away my tears,

Gingerbread to ease my fears.

You gave the gift of life to me

And then in love, you set me free.

I thank you for your tender care,

For deep warm hugs and being there.

I hope that when you think of me

A part of you, you'll always see.

—*Author unknown*

Showing Our Love on Mother's Day

* Your mother makes meals for you every day. How about serving her breakfast in bed?

* Write a poem or letter to your mother. Begin with "I Love You Because…" It can be a very long list!

* Do you have a special grandmother, stepmother, aunt, or sister? Show your love by giving her flowers or a card.

* Do you know someone from another country? Ask if he or she celebrates a special holiday for mothers. Ask what the holiday customs are.

* Is there a home for older people in your community? See if you can visit on Mother's Day. Bring cards or flowers for the women. Ask them to tell you about their lives.

* Try out a new idea: Every day is a day to show Mom how much you appreciate her!

Making French Toast

(For Mom's Special Breakfast in Bed)

What you need:

2 eggs

³/₄ cup milk

¹/₂ teaspoon vanilla

1 teaspoon sugar

6 slices of bread

Cooking spray

Fresh strawberries

Directions

1. Mix the eggs, milk, vanilla, and sugar in a bowl. Using a fork, whisk (stir quickly) the ingredients.
2. Dip each slice of bread into the mixture so that both sides are coated.
3. Spray a skillet with cooking spray, and allow it to preheat on the stove top[*] for a few seconds.
4. Using tongs or a spatula, place one slice of bread on the skillet.
5. Occasionally turn the bread over, and continue cooking until each side is golden brown. Repeat with the other five slices.
6. Finally, arrange the French toast on a plate. Top with sliced strawberries.
7. Bring your breakfast creation to your mom in bed. Be sure to share with the rest of your family, too!

[*]*Have an adult help you operate the stove.*

Making a Mother's Day Gift Box

Here's a gift your mom is sure to love on her special day.

What you need:
A shoe box or other small box
Markers, paints, crayons, stickers,
    wrapping paper, and glitter for decorating
Paper
Glue
Ribbon
Small wrapped presents
    (some examples: coupons for help around the house,
    candy, tea bags, small soaps, cards)

Directions
1. Decorate the outside of the box using markers, paint, crayons or any of the other decorating supplies you choose.
2. Fill the box with the small presents you have chosen.
3. Write a schedule for when you would like her to open each gift. This will be easy if you label each gift with a number.
4. Put the cover on the box and tie it closed with a ribbon.

Now you're ready for a day filled with gift-giving fun. Happy Mother's Day!

Glossary

ancient—from the distant past

carnation—a flower with fluffy petals

goddess—a female god

national—relating to a country

proverb—a wise saying

stepmothers—women who become mothers after marrying men who already have children

tangible—touchable; made of material things

traditional—following long-held customs

Learn More

Books

Eick, Jean, and Kathleen Petelinsek (illustrator). *Mother's Day Crafts*. Mankato, MN: The Child's World, 2011.

May, Eleanor, and M.H. Pilz (illustrator). *The Best Mother's Day Ever*. New York: Kane Press, 2010.

Rockwell, Anne F., and Lizzy Rockwell (illustrator). *Mother's Day*. New York: HarperCollins, 2004.

Wing , Natasha, and Amy Wummer (illustrator). *The Night Before Mother's Day*. New York: Grosset & Dunlap, 2010.

Web Sites

Visit our Web site for links about Mother's Day and other holidays:

childsworld.com/links

Note to Parents, Teachers, and Librarians: We routinely verify our Web links to make sure they are safe and active sites. So encourage your readers to check them out!

Index